CONCRETE
KIDS

AMYRA LEÓN

PENGUIN WORKSHOP

for Elva

Alex, Zoe, Gabriel & Izzy

PENGUIN WORKSHOP
An Imprint of Penguin Random House LLC, New York

Penguin supports copyright. Copyright fuels creativity, encourages diverse voices, promotes free speech, and creates a vibrant culture. Thank you for buying an authorized edition of this book and for complying with copyright laws by not reproducing, scanning, or distributing any part of it in any form without permission. You are supporting writers and allowing Penguin to continue to publish books for every reader.

The publisher does not have any control over and does not assume any responsibility for author or third-party websites or their content.

Text copyright © 2020 by Amyra León. Illustrations copyright © 2020 by Penguin Random House LLC. All rights reserved. Published by Penguin Workshop, an imprint of Penguin Random House LLC, New York. PENGUIN and PENGUIN WORKSHOP are trademarks of Penguin Books Ltd, and the W colophon is a registered trademark of Penguin Random House LLC. Manufactured in China.

Visit us online at www.penguinrandomhouse.com.

Library of Congress Cataloging-in-Publication Data is available upon request.

ISBN 9780593095195

10 9 8 7 6 5 4 3 2 1

concrete kids

For Harlem & its angels

This is for the concrete kids.

The kids with a melanin kiss. The kids drenched in poverty.
The kids who are told to cut their hair, to tame their tone.
The kids who are told to shorten their names and
disappear their tongues.
The kids who are told they will amount to nothing.
The smart kids who are told they are problematic.
The problematic kids who are told they are stupid.
The kids who are taking care of their families in
between extracurriculars. The kids who cannot go to
extracurriculars because they are taking care of their
families. The stoop kids. The hungry kids. The thirsty kids.
The foster kids. The kids who aged out of the system.
The missing kids. The homeless kids. The kids in jail.
The kids awaiting trial. The innocent kids. The kids who
never got to be kids. The kids navigating the violence of
hands. The kids who are being taught to fear themselves.
The kids who refuse. The kids in gangs. The kids thinking
about joining gangs. The kids who started them.
The adults they became. The adults who wait for the blood
to dry out in the sun with the laundry.

The kids who bury the adults.

The adults who bury the kids.

The angels they became. The angels they will become.

More specifically—this is for the boy in the white tee and the breath I saw escape him.

gardenias

The thing about things that drown
Is that they never learn to breathe right
No one ever told them
Of a life
Without strain
A constant choking
Begging for permission
To remain
Limbless in limbo
Calling on the Good Lord
For some ease
A terrifying permission
Comes with youth
The way our bodies
Selflessly unfold
Before the altar
A sacred celebration
Of gardenias in bloom
Eden welcoming the ruin

I was born somewhere in New York City on May 15, 1992.
I do not know the time of day or
recall the scent of birth, but I am sure I arrived screaming
like everyone else.

pigment

All of me is brown

My eyes, my hair

My skin

I do not know   My father

The source   is a figment

of melanin   of imagination

I have never met him

Barbie looks like my mother

Who does not look like me

Blond hair blue eyes

And a White body

My reflection

Betrays easily

As I yearn

for pieces of her

To stare back at me

there is love

there is love

there is love

there is questioning

There are no Black Barbies

My mother hand paints

them brown

I do not know

If this makes me

Feel better

There's no way to

Fabricate reality

So we might as well

Let barbie be

Barbie

kelly be Kelly

 9

& ken be Ken

I do not

Need to

Be White

Like *her*, like *them*

To love the skin

That I am in

taken

It is December
We are on the 6 train to Parkchester
Barely old enough to speak
feet swinging above the world
I play hide-and-seek
With strangers
As the lights on the train flicker

My mother
Gives me a Kelly doll,
an early Christmas gift
In excitement
I beg for more
She says no
I persist
She slaps me
This is the beginning
To the end of everything

Two women in pantsuits

Call the police

A few stops later

They take me

Apparently

They are

Social workers

Perhaps they smell

The vodka on her tongue

Or know the demons

we are running from

Regardless

My mother

Leaves alone

And I wake

In a group home

loose noose

'round my neck
'round my mama's breast
'round my brain
'round my mama's too

'round my wrists and my breath
'round my ankles and my dreams

loose noose got me
itching at the seams

wondering if I will defy gravity
or if it will defy me

loose noose
'round my name
'round my history

'round my reflection
'round my ancestry

'round my limbs
'round my marrow

'round today
'round tomorrow

Round and round
it goes

loose until
its knot

loose until
The world
it stops

The Little Flower waiting room knows me all too well. It is an awful shade of yellow with broken toys and trash littered everywhere. The sound of children and their mamas crying, social workers screaming, and phones ringing. I come here twice a month to see my birth mother in a small room with no doors and too many chairs for the two of us. We crouch together and attempt normalcy as the chaos continues on either side of us.

Without fail she strips me naked in a corner and scans my body for signs of abuse. She often discovers what she is looking for, then gives me a toy to play with as she reports her findings. I know this is her way of showing love but I wish we could just sit, talk, maybe even play a game like we used to.

I have long forgotten what home feels like and have stopped dreaming of the day my birth mother will take me there. I have moved so many times, I no longer unpack my bags. I have stopped trying to be liked by the other foster children, stopped trying to be friends with the kids at school. It makes no sense to get attached to anyone or anything when *in the blink of an eye everything can change*.

I have cultivated a safe kinship with silence. My social workers no longer ask questions. I am sure they are tired of hearing truths they do not have the power to change. My teachers see the bruises on my body and know I am stealing food from the lunchroom, but they too know that our silence will save us both a lot of time.

The older you get in care the less likely you are to get adopted. I see the worry in my social worker's eyes because she knows this. The more you've experienced, the less likely you are to forget. Every family wants a blank slate but when you have danced in the shadows I've known, everyone is scared of the day you will finally react. They read my file and assume the wars I have fought have left wounds that are bound to open. They fear they will not be able to love me out of the trenches.

It seems like everyone else has come to the conclusion that my future is somehow damned and not worth fighting for. If I didn't love myself, I would probably agree with them.

When I started court-mandated therapy and everyone realized I had no intentions of speaking, they gave me a notebook and crayons.

They told me to draw, I chose to write.

...

There is magic in a blank page

the way it promises me a future

even if only for the next five minutes.

I can start here

and

end anywhere

I can be anyone

Including the person

I already am

elastic

My reflection has never been easy

When I did not see my mother

And had no father to compare

I had to learn to see who was really

There

Staring back at me

Had to love her more than I loved anybody

Foster care forces you to

Befriend the temporary

To assimilate constantly

To pretend you have

No dreams, no memory

So I fell in love with the

Ephemeral nature

Of *being*

Each sunrise

Reflected in my eyes

Is a hymn

To the moment

Each sunset

A reminder

That time

Like light

Can shift

That the sacred

Nature of breath

Is all I need

To manifest

The life

They say

I'll never live

Oh to know

A love like this

Everlasting and malleable

A love that will forever

Become the light

In the uninhabitable

we are all saints

Self-love

Is the process

Of becoming

Safe in your body

Saying hello to the

Softest parts of you come morning

Behind the ears, the knees,

Under your chin, the soles of your feet

Creating a temple

Out of your skin

Laughing with yourself

In the mirror

Until you feel

Whole again

Basking in

The sacred nature

Of your heart beat

And your ribs

Vaseline and scripture

Forever kept on your lips

We are all saints

It is merely a matter

Of worship

madre mia

I move to Harlem two days before my eighth birthday.

I have nothing but a backpack and a bright pink diary with
Barbie on it. We get off the 2 train at 110th Street and there
it is: Central Park. I have only seen it in rom-coms starring
White people, I didn't even know it went all the way up to
Harlem! The trees are taller than any I have ever seen, they
embrace the sky with ease, they are free in ways I dream
to be. The walk from Lenox to 5th is short in distance but
takes an eternity because my new mother knows everyone
and everyone knows her. We stop a million times before
we turn right onto 109th Street, it is like walking with
royalty. As we turn onto 5th you can see the Twin Towers
lit up like diamonds in the sky. Before we make it to the
front door, I know Harlem will be my home. Something
about it feels right, feels safe, feels like I don't have to lie
and make up a distant relative to justify my mysterious
arrival. There is a sense of peace in me walking down these
streets with someone everyone seems to love. I want to
love her and be loved by her. I want to one day walk these
streets on my own with *my* name on their tongues.

Elva Rosa León
Proud Boricua
With the head scarf on
Silk painted red
Chains cascading
Across her chest
Nicky's wedding band
Next to St. Lazarus

Hands littered in rings
and pointed gel tips
A wrist of evil eyes and Saints
San Pascual, San Francis de Assisi,
and Guadalupe

Altar by the door
Ellegwa beneath the sink
Mommy surrounds herself
With holy things
She dares me to believe
In what I do not see

Veins dancing visibly
To the ocean of her heart
Forever ready to wash the blood

Out of anything and consider it clean
To name the impossible
and consider it seen

She too
Is capable
Of baptism

Capable of
Relinquishing one
Of their sins

I suppose that is
What mothers do

Forgive on behalf of God
They are both capable of giving life

A mother is not always the one who births you,
sometimes it is the person who raises you. I know I may
not be your birth mother, but you are my daughter.

She said this to me with a smile in her eyes and for the
first time in my life all of the worry left my body. She is the
only other person I have felt comfortable calling Mommy.
Everyone else has made me feel like a burden but she
makes me feel easy to love.

new shit

i get new shit

three times a year

probably

shouldn't

call it shit

considering

it is all i got

and what i got

ain't shit

at least

to me

but three times a year

i get new shit

christmas

easter

and my

birthday

thank god for dem holy days

one birthday is not enough

for the ever-changing needs

of my growing body

'round the resurrection

we are all on our best behavior

knowing that anything

can compromise

the long-awaited day

when we walk into

Regines on 116th Street

and walk out with

more than panties

birthdays are simple

but they are my favorite

it's the one time a year

i get a new pair of shoes

and if i am lucky a new piece of

jewelry from mommy's friend

who sells gold and silver pieces

outside the Western Union on 2nd Ave

christmas

is the turn up of the year

it ain't just jesus's birthday

it's everyone's

though jesus wasn't born

in december, neither was i

and lord am i grateful

that we celebrate it

in winter

i always get

socks, bras, pads, pajamas,

and whatever school supplies i need

most of the kids in the fam be upset

that we never get toys

but i live for essentials
ain't nothing more satisfying
than a matching pair of socks
a new journal
and knowing that you and
all of your cousins
will have twin
pajama sets
to rock all
christmas break

it is the only time of year
when everyone seems to gather
there is a lot to mourn
but more to be grateful for
dance-offs to ref
and standard viewings of
The Grinch, Selena, Home Alone,
and The Nightmare Before Christmas
i do not know how Selena
became our christmas classic
but we forever

bidi bidi bom bom

our way into the new year

it is the only time

when food is in abundance,

and trust,

not one ounce of it

goes to waste

la marqueta

electric saturday's in el barrio

caminando con mi madre

bailando con el sol

la marqueta

a weekly celebration

of Puerto Rico

La Isla de Encanta

fresh bacalao

dominoes

bomba y plena

we can't help

but eat as we go

sugar cane, yucca, aloe vera

tomato, aguacate y quenepas

this is our daily bread

this is our reminder

it is more than a market

it is our culture

it is generations

of laughter

echoing

in the tunnels

somewhere

between here and there

where all our family

gathers

infestation

There is a war
One that suffocates language
before it has a chance
to escape us
One that aims
to shift the DNA
Of our kingdom
as we sleep

Come morning
They will call our confusion
Amnesia
Call our amnesia
A joke
Rewrite the reality
And tell us
what we need to know
As their quiet laughter
Dismantles
The walls of our home

There is a war

Entire neighborhoods

Entire countries

Entire generations

Will die

Fighting

There will be blood

There will be blood

There will be blood

Everyone knows

the scent

Will eventually

Cradle its way

Into our nostrils

The same way

Roaches become

a part of the family

And the entrée

They sold the empty lot on Madison, where we often play
and devour chubby's and peanut chews after school.
The drilling has begun and the entirety of 109th Street

is newly infested with cat-rats and roaches—the kind that multiply *and* the kind that fly. Apparently they are turning our little corner of paradise into a condom for the rich—luxury apartments for those who can afford it and a Dunkin Donuts in the lobby for everyone else. America may run on Dunkin but El Barrio runs on Bustelo so trust—munchkins and 99 cent iced coffee will never be enough to soften the blow. No one knows how long it will take to build but we all got our eyes on the overgrown lot on 5th and know what's coming.

Despite the scarcity and the occasional hunger, we live in abundance. There is no sense in living otherwise. We are holy in our hand-me-downs and joyous in the pantry line. We never let ourselves get consumed with what we do not have, we rejoice in the reality of what we do. There is no way to discuss Harlem's wonder without its struggle and no way to mention its struggle without its celebration.

Depending on the day, you could find Harlem somewhere between Eden and a war zone.

BLINK

In the blink of an eye

Everything can change

Blink.

Black car.

Blink.

Windows roll down.

Blink.

Music louder now.

Blink.

Shots.

Blink.

Too many.

Blink.

His friends and all their limbs running.

Blink.

His body hits the floor.

Blink.

It is summer in Harlem again. The block is hot(ter than usual)
and everyone's skin is glowing. A sixteen-year-old boy has
just been shot. I am thirteen. I am locked outside of my
building, grasping my Tropical Fantasy for dear life, trying
not to pee myself. My friend disappeared the second
she heard the first pop. I, *still*, in limbo trying to decide
whether it was a firework or a gunshot, after the Fourth of
July they're indecipherable. It was a gunshot. It was many.
I wished myself away and closed my eyes in hopes that
whoever just shot the boy in the white tee—
wouldn't be looking to clean up any witnesses.

Blink.

*Mommy they shot a boy downstairs. He was young but older
than me and all his friends ran away and I was locked out
and I saw them do it—what if they come back for me—
he is lying there on the concrete, what if they come back for
me. What if he dies. Mommy. I saw them do it. They shot
him, there is blood everywhere, they shot him and all his
friends ran away. They shot him. What if he dies, Mommy.
What if he dies?*

Blink.

I am in my living room. I do not recall how I got here,
but I managed to get into the building and up the five
flights of stairs to my mother, fragile in her skin, watching
novelas on the couch. She lets me cry, she lets me scream
but she eventually turns to me and says,

*"Nena, this happens every day. You are alive, okay. You are
alive. Relax."*

Then shifts her body ever so slightly to face the television.

40

Blink.

I can hear his mother screaming.

It sounds like she is bleeding from her throat.

Her cries are long, her breath is short.

I am in my room crying with her.

Blink.

I find myself in the middle of a prayer, urine fresh down my leg, fear crippling my body, no doubt in my mind that he is dead.

I hear sirens, a sound that usually riddles my body with anxiety is now a lullaby. Perhaps he is still alive, perhaps they can save him.

The sirens sound and for a second I let myself think that he still has a chance, that his last breath has yet to escape him. I imagine the ambulance doors flying open, five people rushing to his aid—slowly removing the bullets and caressing the wounds, punching him in the chest if they have to, breaking his ribs if they have to, anything to keep him alive— just like they do on TV. I see them attempt everything, I see him come to. I see them lay his body soft on the stretcher, I see them find his mother, she is crying but hopeful, he is bleeding but alive, they rush him to the hospital.

He lives. He lives. He lives.
He lives. He lives. He lives.
He lives. He lives. He lives.
He lives. He lives. He lives.
He lives. He lives. He lives.
He lives. He lives. He lives.

Blink.

I hear sirens and for the first time in my life I pray for them to turn onto our street.

They do not.

The police did not come for four hours.

42

They did not come until there were limbs to collect, when it could have been a life. I do not know why they didn't rush to this like the emergency that it was, like they do on TV, though the survivors on television are always White. I suppose reality is no better. He bled out on the concrete, despite the summer heat, it took three days for the blood to dry. The sound of his mother's screams haunt me from time to time like a song that lives on your tongue that you cannot name. I do not know his name. But I will carry him with me for the rest of my life—a legacy beyond the pavement.

i watch the leaves fall
and the moths fly into the light
the ladybugs' wings are black and white
the birds speak in a language
i swear i understand
i am laying here in the soil
pretending it is sand
bones weightless
defying gravity just like the trees
who never die
when they are cut down or sick
they distribute their nutrients evenly
like Harlem, inheritance flows
through the roots—you see
as they give us all
this tender oxygen to breathe
inhale exhale
i try to stand still enough
to hear my own heartbeat
so it can remind me
that i am alive
and free

I linger in awe of everything

In everything awe lingers

my ancestors rejoice at the syncopation of my breath
they waltz across my eyes as i attempt to rest
Black boys be eternal, they turn to butterflies
then kiss they sisters on they eyes
become the glimmer of hope in our spines
their names roll off our tongues like
amen hallelujah—smoke will always rise,
children of the sun burning burning
burning tides and we wonder why
as jordans and nikes
greet the skyline
they dun exchanged their feet for wings
the architecture
of angels
becoming
ancestry

Black boys be eternal

When they die

They turn to butterflies

Met with the memory of birth

Before they forget

All that they were

legacy

We write our names in the concrete
Just in case mourning comes early
Just in case we start disappearing
Just in case the moon don't shine
And there ain't no melody in our cry
Just the absent ache of becoming

We write our names in the concrete
To claim what is rightfully ours
To manifest a legacy
They said we could never know

To reclaim the history
They tried to silence
The revolution was
Jazz in response to violence

They could not
Take the rhythm

From our bones

They could not

Disintegrate the

Melody in our marrow

Brass and Gospel

Funk, Rock 'n' Roll

They may steal the land

But they will never capture the soul

We write our names in the concrete

Line the track with our heartbeat

Beat beat beating the life

Into the ground where

All our kin seem to be

We write our names in the concrete

Dreaming of the day

We are finally free

free

that thing they say i ain't
that thing i want to be
that thing i can't define
that thing that's choking me

that thing they try to hide
in the narrow of their lies
that thing that burrows deep
'neath the fabric of our lives

that thing that seems to give
that thing that seems to take
that thing that has power
but does not bear a face

that thing that keeps us
hungry and wide-eyed
that thing that keeps the rich
full yet dissatisfied

that thing that keeps the grass
greener only where i am not
that thing that will continue
to bear fruit
as we rot

in the very
sun that birthed us
palms up
awaiting mana

soft nigga

natural disaster

look at me

all holy, breathing

in my

black

in my

brown

skin

breathing ((soft))

breathing ((slowly))

like no one is

chasing

chasing me

like i am

allowed

allowed to be

like ain't no

tomorrows

in question

like i ain't no

existence

to question

like they

ain't no

questions

like *i am*

i am just

i am

soft

i am

holy

breathing

slowly

like i am

just ((allowed to be))

soft

where i grew up niggas wasn't allowed to be soft.
the second their balls dropped they were invited to
become callous soldiers for the family, for the block,
to protect themselves from getting soft nigga beatings,
which i suppose were supposed to be gifts rather than
warnings. where i grew up niggas wasn't allowed to be.
the police would never show up when we called, but they
were always somehow around. we didn't have the words
"stop-and-frisk" in the '90s but we all knew how to get to
Rikers from Harlem. some niggas decided long ago that
no niggas could be soft. *them* niggas must have known
that niggas *soft or not* will one day find themselves in a
situation where they must defend themselves. the only
truth we knew was that *all* niggas had to defend
themselves. *including me.*

if i wasn't a girl
i woulda been a
soft nigga

i didn't like fighting
but i did when i had to

 54

i had to when i did

but otherwise didn't

found myself leaning

into an education

that no one believed in

until i realized they

were right

these books

ain't tell the truth

the history in them

always made us out to be savages

always made us out to be slaves

got us all digesting

a history

that only records

the capture

not the real free

freedom is not

a hope

but a memory

 55

one that will

return to me

sometimes i confuse sirens for laughter

i find myself harmonizing with them

begging God that they don't stop

on my block—that they don't park

in front of my building like they

tend to do

'cause niggas

soft or not

tend to die

in/tension

Raised in tension
With good intentions
Walking contradictions
Curated fiction

Poverty be a different
POV of reality
Looking for the
Things inside of me
That make me *rich*
Ain't no runnin' away
Ain't no tryna be different
No matter how far you go
You never grow out of
Hood politics

I was taught
To worship our music
Our people

If 5th was the mountain

Madison was the steeple

All of us prophets

All of us saints

All of us holy

Simply praying we make it till morning

Our parents cannot

Dictate the way the world sees us

So they teach us

How to walk

In every situation

If you encounter blue

hands up, mouth shut

Raised on henny and disappointment

Don't get caught up

With premature excitement

Be faithful

But keep your prayers

Within reason

Never let the weather

Dictate the season

Loyalty

Is essential

Anything else

Be treason

No matter what

We be the reflection

Of a God worth

Believing

Raised in tension

With good intentions

Walking contradictions

Curated fiction

Keeps me afloat

Long enough

To know

I am living

There is no way to reconcile the intricacies of our survival.
Resilience like jazz cannot be taught.

George died out in the sun today
His blueberry skin glistening
Long after his heart had stopped

My mama is everyone's mama and George was one of her
sons. He loved making sculptures out of things he found in
the street, he also wrote poetry and loved to paint.
He was really tall and thin and his skin was dark as night.
His beard was salt 'n' peppa black and he always wore a
hat. He was a renaissance man and like any other body
born jazz he knew his fair share of struggles—but there
was a quiet smile in his eyes and his laughter would roar
throughout the building. He loved to sing and would
always greet my mother with a story or a song and then
he would come upstairs and have dinner. We didn't have
much but we always had enough to give and George was
always grateful. He was a light in this world, I am glad the
sun was there to greet him as he too became a star.

Johnny died a few weeks ago
The virus consumed
His unwavering light
In the middle of the night
My mother is still crying

My mama is everyone's mama and Johnny was one of her sons. Johnny had a really long ponytail and an undeniable smile. He loved wearing turtlenecks and long trench coats. You always knew when Johnny was coming because he sang himself into every room, forever ready to share stories of his life downtown. If you're born in Harlem you likely stay in Harlem and that is to say within a two-mile radius in any direction of the stoop—so him telling us about downtown was an introduction to an alternate universe. Johnny met mama when he first got diagnosed. Like a lot of other young people his parents kicked him out when they found out about the AIDS and mama welcomed him with open arms. Whenever he was in the hospital we would visit with nothing but holy water and time to give. The virus may have taken his body, but his smile will live in me forever.

born again

That's how niggas die

By accident

For some of them

It's the same way they came in

Accident

It happens so quickly and

The world just keeps turnin'

Like some kind of sick joke

Where no one is laughing

The silence it seeps in

The silence it lingers like

Butchered tongues and bloody mouths

Broken fists

Glistening glistening

Forever shining

Can't tell if we're

Dancing or dying

Tell me something

I don't know

About myself

Tell me

Go 'head

Speak on

My marrow

Speak on the

Name of the

Mother I don't know

Go 'head

Tell me 'bout

Tomorrow

When the sun

Chooses to rest

And the moon

Does not return

Tell me

What you know

'Bout war

On your lips

'Bout the hunger

Like quicksand

That sits at the pit

Of your stomach

Relentless

Tell me what you know

'Bout me

What you

What you

Know 'bout me

All I see

Is worshippers

Confused in their reverence

Afraid that their sins

Will one day know

Penance

Birthmarks

Maps to faces like traces

of places I've never been

Shadows highlighting my kin

Holy in my hand-me-downs

Watch me

Watch me as I

Breathe

in

Breathe

out

Breathe in

Breathe out

Now

Drop

Now

Drop

Now drop

Dead like

You'll come

Again

∞

Black boys be eternal
When they die
They turn into
Butterflies

coat hanger boy

Coat hanger boy

Smiles with teeth

Meant for grindin'

A meat kind of boy

Hangin' from the tree

What a poplar place to be

How metal becomes

The bones of a child

When they're forced

To watch their father

Die & die & die

Again & again

As the world says

Watch this Till

You understand

Grabbin' their

Picnic blankets

And their favorite snack

To watch the public lynching

Of an innocent man

As his name becomes

Another hashtag

Our melanin—

A wink to the

Constant mourning

We do not wear black

Can't take it off

After lunch

After dinner

After they kill us

We ain't nothing but nigger

An afterthought—

A marginalized depiction

Of what God forgot

Can't just decide to be safe

Wake up every day

With the weight of

Racism anvilling on our chests

With a *loose noose*

'Round our neck

There is no escaping this

They made a habit out

Of watching things die

Star gazing—Black bodies

In the night sky

God is nigh

God is here

God is laughing up there

At the family reunion

As Jesus and his sand skin

Prepare the gates

For the welcoming

Fills the basin

With the very water

His sister auntie cousin brother mother father son &

daughter

Been drownin' in

Ready to wash them calloused feet

Of the nigga who died again & again

Waitin' on the world to praise 'em

They been celebratin' our death for 2000 years

We shouldn't be surprised

That they made of us

The sacrifice

Us: tangible

Disciples of the Lord

Got the earth

In our inheritance

Made slaves out of Us

'Cause we the only ones

Who know how to care for it

That don't mean we ain't tired

That don't mean we asked to be

But we is

We here

You're gonna have to kill me

headlines

Sometimes you
Let the thought
Linger too long
A quiet fear of death
Tastes like metal
And your favorite song

You start daydreaming
Of people reposting your death
On social media
Wonder if the general public
Will get to see the "real" you
Worry about the casket costs
Your mama cannot afford
And the police
When they finally knock
On your door
You see your mother's face
When she greets the news

The way laughter

Embraces her sorrow

The way she avoids sleep

To delay tomorrow

Another day

Without

lemonade

When life gives you lemons
Make lemonade
Obviously
Then use the skin of the lemon
To make tea
And plant the seeds just in case
They take to the soil

When the milk goes bad
We make cheese

When the Coke is flat
We make broth

If it's in a can
It doesn't expire

When we outgrow our clothes
There's always a cousin

 73

When our food stamps run out
José gives us credit

When they shut off the hot water
There's always a neighbor

When they kill someone you love
Everyone gathers
To carry the
Survivors
Through the night
Until the morning comes

limousines

I've spent most of my childhood
Somewhere in the back of a limo
En route to a cemetery
In Yonkers or Queens
For someones
Who died of
Unnatural causes
That we rarely discuss
The adults cry
As we run around
Waiting for the pastor to
Unite us in prayer
Where they slip in
That all those who lead
A life of sin could be
Forgiven
Us kids
Didn't know
The sin we

Were living in

or the liberation

of forgiveness

But all of our kin

Seem to die

all sacrificial

Drenched in blood

Honestly

I don't know

Where we get

The money

To bury

So many

But I know

No matter

How empty

My stomach is or will be

We will always have enough

For the limo

When the dead are just dead when the dead are just dead

When the dead are just dead when the dead are just dead

When the dead are just dead when the dead are just dead

When the dead are just dead when the dead are just dead

When the dead are just dead when the dead are just dead

When the dead are just dead when the dead are just dead

When the dead are just dead when the dead are just dead

When the dead are just dead when the dead are just dead

When the dead are just dead when the dead are just dead

When the dead are just dead when the dead are just dead

When the dead are just dead when the dead are just dead

When the dead are just dead when the dead are just dead

When the dead are just dead when the dead are just dead

When the dead are just dead when the dead are just dead

When the dead are just dead when the dead are just dead

When the dead are just dead when the dead are just dead

When the dead are just dead when the dead are just dead

When the dead are just dead when the dead are just dead

When the dead are just dead when the dead are just dead

When the dead are just dead when the dead are just dead

Frida Kahlo reminds me of Tupac and Biggie. They expressed their realities regardless of how controversial or difficult it was to face. Our hustle, our Black, our abundance, our love intertwined in the melody. Their art reminds me that the revolution begins with me. It requires me to love myself so much that the darkest parts of my history are worn with pride. It reminds me that I am beautiful regardless of the wars I've known.

Sometimes I go and sit with Ellington on 5th, he's built sky-high in bronze, onlooking Schomburg keeping us all aware that we can do more with our lives than die or work for someone else. He revolutionized jazz, made space for us to be celebrated. When the world caves in and I don't feel like running I go and sit with Duke. I daydream. I imagine what it must be like to walk down the street with all that talent inside of you—all them melodies haunting you with songs that will become your legacy. What it must have been like to collaborate with Nina Simone, Ella Fitzgerald, and Billie Holiday—writing freedom into existence one composition at a time, as Jim Crow laws threatened their lives.

kin

I am

Be

Cause

I am

Be

Cause

They

Were

Be

Cause

Blood

Is both

Liquid

And

Solid

As is

History

If we

Allow it

The fucks the difference between a pigeon and a dove?

Nothing.

eye to eye

see me see you

i see you

i see me in you

you see me

you see threat in me

i see you

i see you in me

you see you

you see holy—thing

you see me

you see disappearing—things

i see me

i see God in me

you see me

you see evil—things

i see you

i see me in you

you see me

you see threat in me

instant recall

On the days your reflection does not appear:

Know your eyes are the color of soil

Your skin the color of sand

Your hair is a universe of curls exploding toward the sky

You are allowed to be soft

Allowed to unclench your fist

To loosen your jaw

To stop holding your breath

To count your vertebrae

To count the stars

To dream

Bigger than yourself

Outside of yourself

You are allowed to think for your self

To question authority

to question your peers

To question the law

To question God

To question your self

There is more to this
Than they made it seem
Do not let them
Diminish your name
Do not let them
Diminish your history
You are allowed
Allowed to be

without you
there would be no world
sure the earth would still exist.
but *without the arrival*
of your breath
There would be no
you
To digest it

my mama said

My love
You are holy
I have led
The life
I have led
So that you
Never have to

get loose

Loose noose

Gets looser

With each

Generation

Soon the

Itch too

Will fade

There

Will be

No sign

Of this

To

Dissect

A history

Written

From

My

Perspective

86

day of rest

the arrival of a

sunday afternoon

in harlem

feels like

the moment the platano hits the oil

the greasing of your scalp

holy rations of pegau

it's arroz con pollo

it's mac and cheese

it's Goya

it's Lawrys

it's all the angels

whose names

we keep

it's when we

forget that we're poor

because we truly

have everything

it's the moment I

start to believe

the margins will diminish

it's the realization

that I am more

than a statistic

it's the smile in

your mother's eyes

as she sleeps

it's the face of every

lucky penny you find

on the street

it's the day after christmas

when everyone is full

its the joy

in the cemetery

as we pour the soil

it's the prayers we

say without words

the love we give

without question

a sunday afternoon

in harlem

is all we need

to keep goin'

morning due

Today what a solemn hymn
Today I woke again

Blood flowing through, my veins
Into the quiet, of the ocean

I dreamt myself alive
And when I opened my eyes
I danced
With my reflection

I cradled the sky

Today what a solemn hymn

Today I woke again

In my holy, in my black skin
Knowing liberation

My hopes are high

Somewhere
With the bird's-eye
Easing the tide

Today
Today
Today
Is the only
Thing I know
For sure
My past
Is water
Under
The bridge
And tomorrow
Is for the angels
To gift
But today
Today

Today

Today, I live

free from

The color red
has never been
free from blood

Veins a river
of sanctuary
Skin peeling back
in the sun

Begging for
Forgiveness
In a language
you do not speak

Fragile and absent
A whimsical misread
Of the air

All spirits in question
Have retired for the night

You ought to rest, kid
They all seem to be

the joke of racism
is choking me
with the reality
that some of us
will fight till we die
& only know rest
in the afterlife

I find myself screaming
at the sun again
Waiting on the revolution
It seems to be
all my kin are dying
Then resurrecting

I've been dancing
I've been dancing
I've been dancing
With my ancestors
In silence

Can you flip the record?

For the record,
I am aware
That the light
Is shifting

That the blood has dried
Out in the sun
With the laundry

That the sound
of your voice
Is drifting
The weight of my soul
Needs some lifting
Been sifting
Through the ash
For a while now
And all I can see
Are reflections of me
running toward a future
I am afraid to greet

The cost of liberation—see

Seems to be

A life of yearning

I so quietly discerning

the taste of captivity

As it embraces me

Like my mother's voice

Come morning

I wish to know

morning without mourning

morning without mourning

I am not afraid of death

Just the way its stench

Seems to linger

The way it always takes

The empty seat

At the dinner table

Without asking

life after life

I too know why the caged bird sings
She has carried the song for centuries
The hymn that unites
All sons
All daughters
The melody that made it
Across the water
The blood
That keeps us
At the seams of everything
Knee-deep in soil
Harmonizing

If time exists
Can we break it?

When I see you again
We'll be different

Butterfly wings
Singing in tandem
With everything

ABOUT US

Prospect Heights Public Library
12 N. Elm Street
Prospect Heights, IL 60070
www.phpl.info

Pocket Change Collective was born out of a need for space. Space to think. Space to connect. Space to be yourself. And this is your invitation to join us.

These books are small, but they are mighty. They ask big questions and propose even bigger solutions. They show us that no matter where we come from or where we're going, we can all take part in changing the communities around us. Because the possibilities of how we can use our space for good are endless.

So thank you. Thank you for picking this book up. Thank you for reading. Thank you for being a part of the Pocket Change Collective.